24 EASY CLASSICAL
SOLOS FOR VIOLA

HARRY HUNT, JR., MFA

ENTERTAINMENT, INC.

24 Easy Classical Solos for Viola
Harry Hunt, Jr., MFA

©2025 Harry Hunt, Jr.

Published by A2G Entertainment Inc.
Chicago, IL
harryhuntjr.com

ISBN: 978-1-954127-43-2 (Paperback)

Printed in the USA
Third Edition

CONTENTS

PLAY-ALONG & DEMONSTRATION TRACKS

To Stream or Download
Click or Visit
<u>harryhuntjr.net/book-ecs-viola</u>

OTHER LINKS

https://sites.google.com/view/book-tracks/viola

(bookmark the links in your browser for quicker access)

1. HOT CROSS BUNS

(Two-bar piano intro)

2. LIGHTLY ROW

(Two-bar piano intro)

3. LULLABY

Brahms

(Two-bar piano intro - pickup starts on beat 3)

4. AU CLAIR DE LA LUNE

(Two-bar piano intro)

5. TWINKLE

(Two-bar piano intro)

6. SCARBOROUGH FAIR

(Two-bar piano intro)

7. OH SUSANNA

Foster

(Two-bar piano intro - pickup starts on beat four)

8. MARRIAGE OF FIGARO

Mozart

(Two-bar piano intro)

9. LONG LONG AGO

Bayly

(Two-bar piano intro)

10. RONDEAU

Mouret

(Two-bar piano intro - pickup starts on beat four)

6
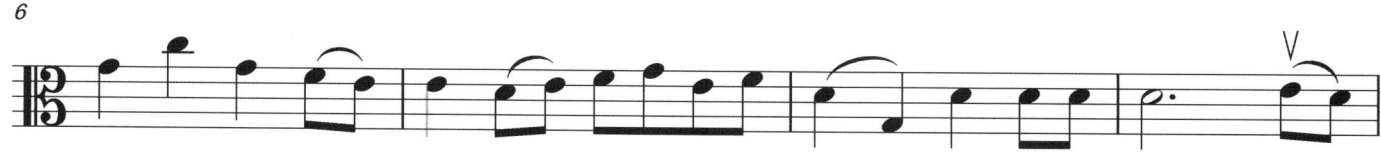

10

14
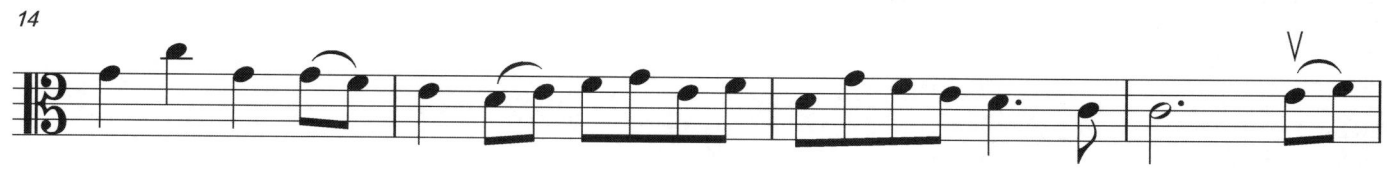

18

22

11. PIANO CONCERTO #3

Beethoven

(Two-bar piano intro)

12. SYMPHONY #7 (2nd Movement)

Beethoven

(Two-bar piano intro)

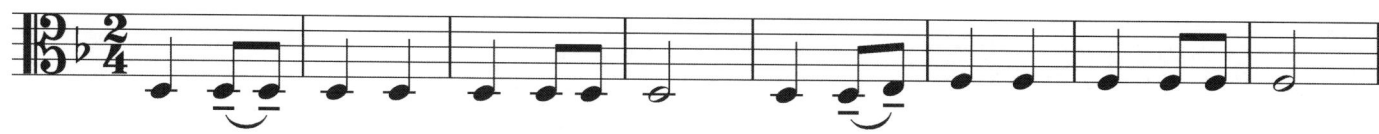

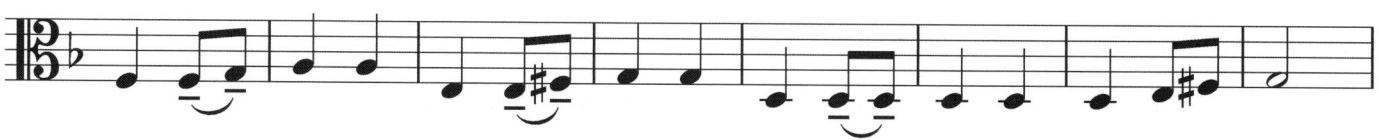

13. GERMAN DANCE

Mozart

(Two-bar piano intro)

14. CHORAL FANTASY

Beethoven

(Two-bar piano intro - pickup starts on beat two)

15. THE HEAVENS ARE TELLING

Haydn

(Two-bar piano intro - pickup starts on beat four)

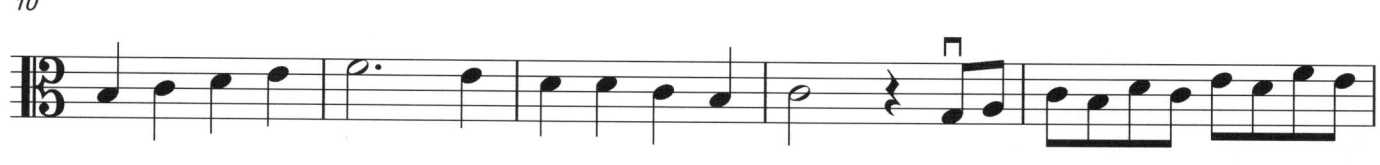

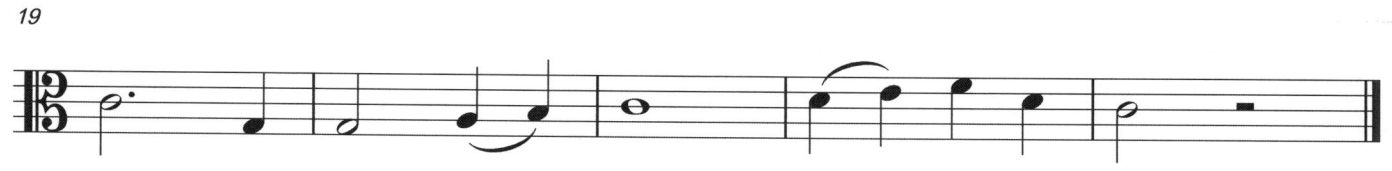

16. BOURRÉE (Water Music)

Handel

(Two-bar piano intro - pickup starts on beat four)

©2024 Harry Hunt, Jr.

17. CARNIVAL OF VENICE

Benedict

(Two-bar piano intro - pickup starts on beat three)

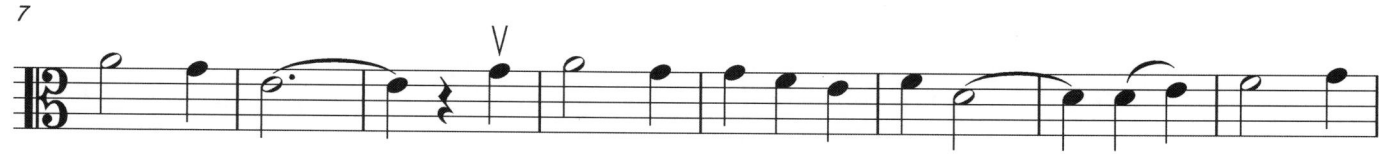

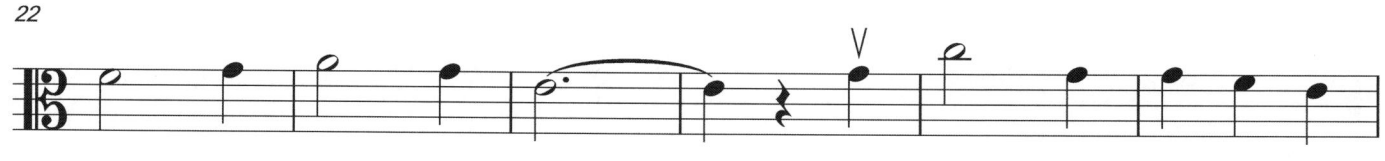

13

18. SONATINA #1

Beethoven

(Two-bar piano intro)

19. LONDONDERRY AIR

(Two-bar piano intro - pickup starts on beat two)

20. BLUE DANUBE

Strauss

(Two-bar piano intro - pickup starts on beat three)

©2024 Harry Hunt, Jr.

21. MINUET I

Bach

(Two-bar piano intro)

22. EINE KLEINE

Mozart

(Two-bar piano intro)

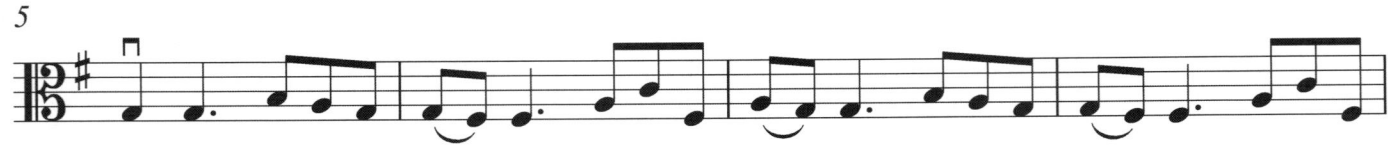

23. SYMPHONY #7 (3rd Movement)

Beethoven

(Two-bar piano intro - pickup starts on beat three)

24. MINUET

Bach

(Two-bar piano intro)

23530194R00015